NUGGETS FOR THE NUMBER NINE:

*The word "NINE" is the ninth
word in the verse 3 times.*

Gen 5:5 And all the days that Adam lived were **nine** hundred and thirty years: and he died.

FYI: this is the first time that the word "nine" appears in the Bible and it just so happens to be the ninth word in the verse.

Gen 17:1 And when Abram was ninety years old and **nine**, the LORD appeared to Abram,

Jdg 4:13 And Sisera gathered together all his chariots, *even* **nine** hundred chariots of iron,…

The word "**NINTH**" is the ninth word in the verse 3 times.

Hag 2:10 In the four and twentieth *day* of the **ninth** *month,* in the second year of Darius,

Mat 20:5 Again he went out about the sixth and **ninth** hour, and did likewise.

Act 10:3 He saw in a vision evidently about the **ninth** hour of the day …

The number nine is the Bible number of "**Fruitfulness**", "**Prayer**", **and the "Holy Ghost"** (9 letters)

Lucifer had 9 stones on his person prior to the fall. Ezek. 28:13

God has assigned a biblical <u>significance</u> to every number in its pages.

Numbers are so important that the Lord even named a book of the Bible: <u>Numbers</u>

These are some <u>observations</u> that I have made concerning the number NINE.

<u>Scoffers</u> of the Bible would snuff at these and call them **"merely coincidental"** because we do not have a verse that says "thus saith the Lord, the number nine has to do with fruitfulness" but through reading, studying and observing plain facts; bible believers have concluded that certain circumstances point to the meaning of numbers by where they appear in scripture and what surrounds the number in context.

For instance:

- Galatians is the **9th book of the N.T.**
- The word **"Galatians" has 9 letters.**
- In Gal. 5:22 we find the **nine manifestations** of the "fruit of the Spirit" COUNT THEM:

But the **<u>fruit</u>** of "<u>the Spirit</u>" (9ltr) is (1) love, (2) joy, (3) peace, (4) longsuffering, (5) gentleness, (6) goodness, (7) faith, **23** (8) Meekness, (9) temperance: against such there is no law.

<u>Do you ever add numbers in an address?</u>

Look at the address of the nine manifestations, in the ninth book called Galatians which just happens to contain nine letters: 5+2+2=**9**, 5+22=27, 3x9 - Just a coincidence I'm sure.

<u>Do you ever count letters in a word?</u>

5:22 contains a **"spiritual" (9 ltrs)** list of the nine manifestations of the "fruit of the Spirit"

The words **"Christian, believers, spiritual, salvation, sacrifice, righteous, dedicated, honorable, separated"**,

<u>Do you ever count the letters in a phrase?</u>

As we see in 1st John 3:1-2: **1** Behold, what manner of love the Father hath bestowed upon us, that we should be called the **<u>sons of God</u>**: **2** Beloved, now are we the **<u>sons of God</u>**, and it doth not yet appear what we

Here are some other connections with "fruitful" items that are probably just coincidental also:

<u>Do you ever count words in a verse?</u>

FYI: this is the **<u>first time</u>** that the word "nine" appears in the Bible and it just so happens to be the ninth word.

Gen 5:5 And all the days that Adam lived were **nine** hundred and thirty years: and he died.

In Gen. **9**:1 Noah is told to "**be fruitful** and multiply" The phrase **"<u>Be fruitful</u>"** appears **nine** times in the Bible.

Who speaks in the bible! The sequence of recorded words by individuals in the bible are:
1-God speaks; Gen. 1:3
2-Adam speaks; Gen. 2:23
3-serpent speaks; Gen. 3:1
4-Eve speaks; Gen. 3:2
5-Cain speaks; Gen. 4:9
6-Lamech speaks; 4:23
7- Gen. 9:25 (seven is the number for perfection, and completeness) Noah speaks, 9:25, he is the 7th different individual to specifically say something that was recorded in the bible. Notice the first words recorded out of Noah's mouth is: 'Cursed be Canaan' verse 25.
In 9:25 he speaks 13 words followed by a period; in verse 26 he speaks 13 words followed by a period; in verse 27 he speaks 13 words followed by a comma and then speaks 6 more words followed by a period. What is the significance of that? The numbers 13 and 6 are joined at the hip to rebellion and man.
Notice that Noah is recorded as speaking 45 words. 45 is 3x3x5, and 5x9.
45 is the 5th hexagonal number;
45 is also the 9th triangular number, that means you add the number 1 through 9 and you get 45.
In verse 25 we see the 6th use of all tenses of the word 'curse'; and

the 6th use of the tense of 'bless';
that is significant because the first words out of Noah's mouth
condemned an entire race of man into servitude.
The King James Holy Bible IS SUPERNATURAL in its design.
The seventh man recorded as speaking in the bible is significant;
he is recorded as speaking only 45 words in his 'scripture' life.

<u>Do you ever count words or phrases in the Bible?</u>

- In Gen 17:1 <u>Abraham was **99** and Sarah **90**</u> when they bare fruit of a miracle baby.

- <u>**9** months</u> for a woman to **produce fruit**.

- Gen. 17:1 the ninth word is NINE.

- The phrase "**ninth hour**" (9 Ltrs) shows up **nine times** in the bible and only in the NT.

Matt. 20:5 is the first time the phrase "**ninth hour**" appears and it just so happens that the ninth word is "ninth". It has to do with harvesting **fruit**!

- the name "**<u>Holy Ghost</u>**" contains <u>**9** ltrs</u> and appears **90** times in the bible

- In John 14:16 the Holy Ghost is given the name "**<u>Comforter</u>**" (**9** ltrs)

- The "<u>King James</u>" (**9** ltrs)

- "<u>Holy Bible</u>" (**9** ltrs) was produced in

- "<u>1611</u>" (1+6+1+1 = **9**)

- There are <u>27 (3x**9**)</u> books in the N.T.
  27 books of the NT 2 + 7 = **9**

In 1st Cor. 12:8-10 we have listed the **9** "**<u>spiritual</u>**" gifts that the **Holy Ghost** (9 ltrs) gives to the body of "**believers**" (**9** ltrs).

CHAPTER 12

1 Now concerning **spiritual** *gifts,* brethren, I would not have you ignorant.

2 Ye know that ye were Gentiles, carried away unto these dumb idols, even as ye were led.

3 Wherefore I give you to understand, that no man speaking by the **Spirit** of God calleth Jesus accursed: and *that* no man can say that Jesus is the Lord, but by the **Holy Ghost**.

4 Now there are diversities of gifts, but the same **Spirit**.

5 And there are differences of administrations, but the same Lord.

6 And there are diversities of operations, but it is the same God which worketh all in all.

7 **But the manifestation of the Spirit is given to every man to "profit" withal.** (that as believers they may be fruitful)

8 For to one is given by the Spirit (1) the word of wisdom; to another the (2) word of knowledge by the same Spirit;

9 To another (3) "faith" by the same Spirit; to another the (4) gifts of healing by the same Spirit;

10 To another the (5) working of miracles; to another (6) **prophecy;** to another (7) **discerning of spirits;** to another (8) *divers* **kinds of tongues;** to another the (9) **interpretation of tongues:**

vs. 28- 13:1 we have 9 items God set in the church in order for it to grow and be fruitful:

28 And God hath set some in the church, **first apostles, secondarily prophets, thirdly teachers,** after that (4) **miracles,** then (5) gifts of **healings,** (6) **helps,** (7) **governments,** (8) diversities of **tongues.** (9) 13:1 **CHARITY.**

- In Acts **9:1-9** (9vs) Paul, the most fruitful Christian in the bible, was saved.

- In Romans **9:9** Paul mentions the miracle birth of Isaac by Abraham (**99**) and Sarah (**90**).

- 1st Cor. **9** has 27 (**3x9**) verses and the entire chapter is admonishing the believers in Corinth to bestow their labour (fruit) on those who do the spiritual work of.

- 2nd Cor. **9** the entire chapter is concerning our bounty given to help those believers back in Jerusalem who were under great persecution.

"NINE" is the ninth word in the verse 3 times.
Gen 5:5 And all the days that Adam lived were **nine** hundred and thirty years: and he died.
FYI: this is the first time that the word "nine" appears in the Bible and it just so happens to be the ninth word.
Gen 17:1 And when Abram was ninety years old and **nine**, the LORD appeared to Abram,

FYI This is the 9th time the word nine appears in scripture and it just so happens to be the ninth word in the verse, Jdg 4:13 And Sisera gathered together all his chariots, *even* **nine** hundred chariots of iron,

"NINTH" is the ninth word in the verse 3 times.
Hag 2:10 In the four and twentieth *day* of the **ninth** *month,* in the second year of Darius, came the word of the LORD by Haggai the prophet, saying,
Matt. 20:5 Again he went out about the sixth and **ninth** hour, and did likewise.
Act 10:3 He saw in a vision evidently about the **ninth** hour of the day an angel of God coming in to him, and saying unto him, Cornelius. (9ltr) His works bore **fruit** and God got the gospel to him.

- **Matt.27 We see the first fruit of Salvation (9lts) after Jesus was crucified (9lts) Centurion (9lts), 27 (3x9) 50-54 (6x9)**

The King James Bible is supernatural in its conception and its content.

Genesis 1:3, "<u>Let there be light</u>" the words light and lights appears **13** times in chapter One. Light was present four days before the sun was created; see Psa. 74:16
Words recorded by the first seven speakers:

God, the first speaker recorded in the bible: God speaks **343** words to creation, which is 7x7x7; God speaks **183** (3x61) words to Adam.

Adam, the 2nd recorded speaker in the bible; speaks **47 (14th prime)** words concerning the creation of Eve, and his defense to God in 2:23, 3:16.

The serpent, the 3rd recorded speaker in the bible, speaks **46** words to Eve.

Eve; the 4th recorded speaker in the bible, speaks 44 words to the serpent, and 8 words to God (**44+8=52, 4x13**).

God speaks **37 (the 12th prime)** words to Eve.
God speaks **63 (3x3x7)** to the serpent.

God speaks **121** (11x11) words to Cain; the 26th word is the first use of the word; SIN.

Cain, the 5th recorded speaker in the bible, speaks **65 (5x13)** words to God concerning the murder of Abel.

Lamech the 6th recorded speaker in the bible speaks **38** words to his wives.

In Genesis 6:13 we have the Lord God speaking to Noah for the first time in the bible. In verse 13-22 God speaks **278** words, in 7:1-4 God speaks **111** words to Noah, that equals: 278+111=389 words. 389 is the 77th prime number, God works in 7s even in condemning the world. 7- (seven is the number for perfection, and completeness) Noah the 7th recorded speaker in the bible 9:25, he is the 7th different individual to specifically say something that was recorded in the bible. Notice the first words recorded out of Noah's mouth is: 'Cursed be Canaan' verse 25.

In verse 25 he speaks 13 words followed by a period; in verse 26 he speaks 13 words followed by a period; in verse 27 he speaks 13 words followed by a comma and then speaks 6 more words followed by a period. What is the significance of that? The numbers 13 and 6 are joined at the hip to rebellion and man.

Notice that Noah is recorded as speaking 45 words. 45 is

3x3x5, and 5x9.

45 is the 5th hexagonal number;

45 is also the 9th triangular number, that means you add the number 1 through 9 and you get 45.

In verse 25 we see the 6th use of all tenses of the word 'curse'; and the 6th use of the tense of 'bless';

that is significant because the first words out of Noah's mouth condemned an entire race of man into servitude.

The King James Holy Bible IS SUPERNATURAL in its design.

The seventh man recorded as speaking in the bible is significant; he is recorded as speaking only 45 words in his 'scripture' life.

Gen 5:5 The first time the word **"nine"** (fruitfulness) appears in the bible and it just happens to be the **9th** word in the verse; the first time the word **"ninth"** appears in the New Testament it also is the ninth word in the verse **Matt 20:5,** it is also the first use of the phrase "ninth hour" which just so happens to show up **nine** times in the bible and is **9** letters.

Genesis 6:9 (man + fruit bearing or fruitful) the name Noah appears 3 times in this verse, the 6th, 7th, and 8th time that his name appears in scripture; the number 6 is the number for "man", 7 is the number for "perfection", 8 is the number for a "new beginning", 9 is the number for "fruitfulness".

The 6th time his name appears the context is related to his **human** "generations" in other words; what his body had generated: the 7th time his name appears it says that God declares him **"just"** and **"perfect"** in his generations i.e.; his genealogy was not mixed with fallen angels: the 8th time it appears. Noah begins something "new" he walked with God: and the 9th mention (verse 10) is him being "fruitful" and "generating fruit" of his loins, Shem, Ham, and Japheth.

The name "Noah" appears 39 (3x13): he was the damnation

of every man on the earth when he entered the ark. The number 13 is seldom a good number.

Noah and Enoch (Genesis 5) are the only two persons who were said to "walk with God" we must take this literally.

Genesis 7:6 Noah was 'six' hundred years old', (7-complete + 6man; six is one number short of God's mark of perfection, 7+6=13) here is the first use of the number "**six**" in scripture and it just happens to be in a verse numbered **six** which also just happens to appear exactly 36 (6x6) verses after the translation of Enoch in Genesis 5:24. Enoch is a type of the Raptured Church age saints prior to the tribulation (flood) period of the end times.

Genesis 7:7 (complete + complete) **"And Noah went in, and his sons, and his wife, and his sons' wives with him, into the ark, because of the waters of the flood".** The word "flood" is the **26th** word (2x13) of the verse an ominous placement to say the least.

You can't get any words more fitting for a 7:7, than the **complete** judgment upon all of the sinners on the earth. When Noah entered the ark, he condemned every human being that was left to die in his own sins; without rescue, without safety, or without life. 2nd Peter 3:9; ...the Lord ... "is not willing that any should perish but that all come to repentance"

FYI:

The first seven persons who speak in the bible! The sequence of recorded words by individuals in the bible are:

1st -God speaks; Gen. 1:3

2nd -Adam speaks; Gen. 2:23

3rd -serpent speaks; Gen. 3:1

4th -Eve speaks; Gen. 3:2

5th -Cain speaks; Gen. 4:9

6th -Lamech speaks; 4:23 The 6th person recorded as saying something in the bible, Lamech was a murderer, and a whoremonger, polygamist.

7th – NOAH, **Gen. 9:25** (seven is the number for perfection, and completeness) Noah speaks, 9:25, he is the 7th different individual to specifically say something that was recorded in the bible. Notice the first words recorded out of Noah's mouth is: **'Cursed be Canaan'** verse 25. In verse 25 he speaks **13 words** followed by a period; in verse **26** (2x13) he speaks **13 words** followed by a period; in verse 27 he speaks **13 words** followed by a comma and then speaks **6 more words** followed by a period. What is the significance of that? The numbers; 13, and 6 are joined at the hip to rebellion and man.

Notice that Noah is recorded as speaking **45** words. 45 is 3x3x5, and 5x9.

45 is the 5th hexagonal number;

45 is also the 9th triangular number, that means you add the number 1 through 9 and you get 45.

In verse 25 we see the 6th use of all tenses of the word 'curse'; and the 6th use of the tense of 'bless';

that is significant because the first words out of Noah's mouth condemned an entire Hamite race of man into servitude.

The **seventh** man recorded as speaking in the bible is significant; he is recorded as speaking only **45** words in his 'scripture' life.

The King James Holy Bible IS SUPERNATURAL in its design.

Genesis 9;

Nine is the bible number for fruitfulness, fruit bearing and the like.

The word "life" in all of its tenses appears 9x in Genesis 9. (Life, lived, lives, liveth, and living)

Galatians (**9** letters) is the **ninth** book of the NT and in Galatians 5:22 we find the nine manifestations of the "fruit of the Spirit".

The address of the nine manifestations in Galatians the 9th book of NT is 5+2+2=**9**;

Or 5+22=27 (3x9)

Here are some "fruitful" items that are associated with the number nine.

There are 27 (3x**9**) books in the N.T. in which we find the fruit of the gospel.

"Be fruitful" appears **nine** times in the Bible.

The phrases "Bare fruit or bear fruit" contain 9 ltrs and appears 9x in scripture.

Genesis 9:9-17 the Noahic covenant consists of **9** verses were Noah is told to "be fruitful and multiply".

It takes **9** months for a woman to produce fruit of a child.

Genesis 17 Abraham was 99 and Sarah 90 when they produced a miracle baby named Isaac.

The name "Holy Ghost"; **9** letters appears **90** (10x9) times in the bible. He is named the "Comforter" (**9** ltrs) in John 17.

The "King James" (**9** ltrs) "Holy Bible" (**9** ltrs) was produced in "1611" (1+6+1+1 = **9**).

In 1st Corinthians 12:8-10 we have listed the **9** gifts of the Holy Spirit to the body of "believers" (**9** ltrs), in the same chapter in vs. 28 we see the 9 functions of the New Testament church; first Apostles, prophets, teachers, miracles, healings, helps, governments, diverse tongues, and 13:4 Charity.

Count the letters in the word's **salvation, Christian, righteous, sacrifice, believers, dedicated, honorable, separated, sanctuary and crucified** they all have to do with a fruitful spirit filled life.

Genesis 9:1 Noah is told by God to "be fruitful"; which appears 9 times in the bible and multiply, and REPLENISH (9 ltrs,) the earth; replenish was the same word used when God gave Adam and Eve the command in Genesis 1:28.

Let's look at the similarities of Adam and Noah.

*Adam has three sons – Noah has three sons.

*Adam was told to replenish the earth – Noah was told to replenish the earth.

*Just before Adam was commanded to replenish the earth there was a flood. - Just before Noah was commanded to replenish the earth there was a flood.

*Adam was naked in a garden – Noah was naked in a garden.

*Adam took of the forbidden fruit – Noah partook of the forbid den fruit.

*They are both sole possessors of the earth.

*They both have a direct commission from God.

*They both replaced races that God did not want controlling the earth.

*One of Adam's sons was a type of Christ (Able), one was a type of the Antichrist (Cain), one of Noah's sons was a type of Christ (Shem) and one was a type of the Antichrist (Ham).

Genesis 9:7, God spoke the words "be fruitful" to four different men, **Adam**; Genesis 1:22 to produce mankind, **Noah**; Genesis 9:1 to repopulate the earth with mankind, **Jacob**; Genesis 25:11 to populate the nation of Israel, and to the **disciples**; John 15, to go and be fruitful producing a new generation of born-again people. Psa. 22:30.

Genesis 9:9, (fruitfulness + fruitfulness) the word COVENANT appears seven (complete or perfect) times in chapter nine; the seventh word in 9:9 is "covenant".

There are nine verses (9-17) describing this covenant; the **thirteenth** (the number which represents evil-wicked-rebellion, etc) word in the verse is "**SEED**" where the fruit of the body originates and is under the curse of the fall.

"Be fruitful" appears 9x in the bible. "Life" in all of its tenses appears 9x in chapter 9.

Genesis 9:25 Noah cursed Canaan, the son of Ham, for what Ham had done to him, Noah could not curse Ham because God had pronounced blessing on him in 9:1.

The curse consisted of **thirteen** (the number for evil-wicked, rebellion) **words**. Noah curses Canaan to be a "**servant of servants**" to Shem (Jewish race) and Japheth (Caucasian race).

This just happens to be the **6th** use of all of the tenses of the word "**curse**".

FYI:

Who speaks when in the bible! The sequence of recorded

words by individuals in the bible are:

#1-God speaks; Gen. 1:3

#2-Adam speaks; Gen. 2:23

#3-Serpent (Satan) speaks; Gen. 3:1

#4-Eve speaks; Gen. 3:2

#5-Cain speaks; Gen. 4:9

#6-Lamech speaks; 4:23

#7-Noah, (seven is the number for perfection, and completeness) Noah speaks in 9:25, he is the 7th different individual to specifically say something that was recorded in the bible. Notice the first words recorded out of Noah's mouth is: 'Cursed be Canaan' in verse 25.

Notice the sequence of words spoken by Noah as recorded in verse 25: he speaks 13 words followed by a period; in verse 26 he speaks 13 words followed by a period; in verse 27 he speaks 13 words followed by a comma, and then he speaks 6 more words followed by a period. What is the significance of that? The numbers 13 and 6 are joined at the hip for rebellion and fallen man.

Three is the number of the trinity, the Godhead, and everything breaks down to three, for example: Time is past-present-future, Elements is air-water-land, Measurements is short-tall-middle, Directions is up-down-sideways, everything that God did is centered around the number three.

Notice that Noah is recorded as speaking 45 words in these 3 verses. 45 (4+5=9) is 3x3x5, and 5x9.

45 is the 5th hexagonal number;

45 is also the 9th triangular number, that means you add the numbers 1 through 9 and you get 45.

In verse 25 we see the 6th use of the tenses of the word **'curse'**; and the 6th use of the tense of **'bless'**; that is significant because the first words out of Noah's mouth condemned an entire race of man into servitude. Cursed be Canaan, a servant of servants.

The King James Holy Bible IS SUPERNATURAL. The seventh man recorded as speaking in the bible is significant; he is recorded as speaking only 45 words in his 'scripture' life.

Gen. 12:10 The word "famine" and "famines" occurs a total of **99** (11x9 a tribulation of fruit) times; and the word "dearth" occurs **8** times in the bible.

Genesis 15:9, (15=3xdeath, nine is fruit), the word 'covenants' is 9 letters, we have 5 (number for death) animals to be sacrificed for the unconditional blood covenant between Abram and God. Whenever you see a 'covenant' in the bible then you will see bloodshed, a covenant is not ratified except by blood. The NT covenant was by the blood of the Lord Jesus Christ who TOOK AWAY the sins of the world Hebrews 9.

The 3 animals were divided, making 6 pieces, the two fowl were not divided but left whole, making 8 pieces. Eight is the number of new beginnings, so the way the sacrifices were laid out, appears as a cross: three over against one another, and the fowls placed on either side of the divided pieces. A picture of the blood covenant that God was to bring about by the cross of the Lord Jesus Christ. The number three appears 3 times in the verse, 3 is the number for the 'Godhead'; found 3 times in scripture, and 3x3 or God x God is Fruit. God is about to give life to a dead man, in order to bring forth a nation of his own.

Genesis 16:11 the first mention of the word "**Ishmael**" (God hears) is in the same verse with the first use of the word "**affliction**". Ishmael was named before birth; **there are nine men that are named before birth:** the phrase "call his name." appears at the naming of: Ishmael, (Gen. 16:11; Isaac, (Gen. 17:19); Josiah (1st Kgs 13:2), Immanuel, (Isa. 7:14), (*a prophecy of the Lord Jesus Christ, fulfilled in Matthew 1:21-23*), Mahershalalhashbaz, (Isa. 8:3); King Cyrus (Isa. 45:1), Jezreel, (Hosea 1:4); Loammi, (Hosea 1:9), John the Baptist, (Luke 1:13), and Jesus (Luke 1:31).

Genesis 17:1 the ninth word is "NINE". The address also equals nine or a multiple of nine; 17+1=18 (2x9) or 1+7+1=9; nine is "fruitfulness" and "fruit bearing" and in 17:6 God promises Abraham to be exceeding fruitful. He fathers Isaac at 99 (nine is the number of fruitful or fruit bearing) years of age, Sarah at 90 (fruit bearing) both ages are significant and are multiples of the number for fruit bearing. The word "seed" appears 7 times in chapter seventeen; the seed is where the fruit is produced. See Ephesians (9th NT book) 5:22, (5+2+2=9) for the 9 fruits of the Spirit and other significant nines.

Genesis 17:10, (1+7+1+0=9; 17+10=27, 3x9) the first use of the word "**circumcised**" in the bible and it is in regard to a covenant between God, Abraham and Isaac, *not Ishmael* or his seed though all of Abraham's family and servants were circumcised. The 'covenant' is always included the shedding of blood. Even in the marriage covenant when a man becomes one flesh his wife, she bleeds, the cloth garment that was bloody was kept as evidence of her virginity. Deut. 22:15-20.

In vs.19-21 God is declaring through circumcision that man's seed is no good, and the judgment upon man's corrupt seed is decapitation of the flesh; from the body (Genesis 3:15 (3+1+5=9, 3+15=18, 2x9) thy seed, her seed) Circumcision relates to the male only because the seed comes from the man. Adams seed was corrupt and for that reason there had to be the VIRGIN BIRTH of the Lord Jesus Christ. This was essential to the saving of the soul of man for had Jesus been born of Joseph, then his blood would have been corrupted just like Adams, therefore, Mary was overshadowed by the Holy Ghost and she conceived, it was God's blood in Jesus *not* Adams. See Acts 20:28.

Genesis 17:15 Sarai gets a new name: "**Sarah**" means "princess"; and she is to be "a mother of nations" even though she is well past the child bearing years. Her son Isaac, a type of Christ, was a miracle baby born to a daddy of 99 years-of-age and a momma of 90 years-of-age. I would say that God performed this miracle to typify his only begotten Son, the Lord Jesus Christ, who was also a miracle baby.

Genesis 17:19 Isaac's birth prophesied.

There are 9 prophecies concerning births in the scripture.

Nine is the number for fruitfulness.

The **nine births** prophesied are: **Isaac**, Gen 17:19, fulfilled in 21:1-3; **Jacob** and **Esau,** the twins; Gen. 25:19-23, fulfilled 25:24-26; **Samson**, Judges 13:2-5, fulfilled 13:24; **Samuel**, 1st Sam. 1:17-18, fulfilled 1:20; The **Shunamite woman's son**, 2nd Kings 4:16, fulfilled 4:17; **John the Baptist**, Luke 1:13-17, fulfilled 1:57-64; **Jesus Christ**, Luke 1:26-33, fulfilled 2:4-7. **Josiah**, 1st Kgs 13:2, **Cyrus**; Isa. 44:28- 45:4

Genesis 21, (the number 3 trinity, x the number 7, complete) here we have the first of the **seven miracle babies** found in scripture: **Isaac,** was the first; he was a miracle baby because his daddy **Abraham, was 99 years old, and his mother Sarah, was 90 years old** at conception, they were both well past the age of giving birth, so, God performed a miracle on them that is a type of the miracle he performed for Mary, the mother of the Lord Jesus Christ, the miracle of the virgin birth.

The ages of the parents of Isaac just happened to be 99 and 90, which is a multiple of the number 9, in the bible the number 9 is the number for "fruit-bearing"; just a coincidence I'm sure.

The nines in the bible all lend to this meaning and it follows through the entire scripture as true. The list is too long to repeat here: take a look at the notes in the 9th book of the NT, Gal. 5:22 (5+2+2=9) (5+22=27 3x9) of the "9 fruits of the Spirit" and follow those notes there.

The other six miracle births are **Joseph,** Genesis 37:3, the greatest type of Christ in the bible, in over 150 places: **Sampson,** Judges 13:1, he is also a type of Christ but a strange type at best:

Samuel, 1st Samuel 1, a great type of Christ who is Israel's Judge, and prophet:

the **Shunamite's son,** 2nd Kings 4:14:
John the Baptist, and **The Lord Jesus Christ** Luke 1.
It could be said that the "eighth" (the number for new beginnings)

miracle birth would be **every born-again Christian,** from Calvary and the Resurrection to the rapture of the church. A miracle of salvation, making every believer a "son of God". (See Gal. 3:26, 1st Peter 1:23 and 1st John 3. In the gospel of John chapter 3, Jesus speaks to "Nicodemus" "the victory of the people" and discusses with him the "new birth", the word "born" just happens to appear 8 times in the chapter. Just a freak coincidence, NOT!

Genesis 24 is the longest chapter in Genesis with 67 verses and coincidentally the Church age is the longest dispensation of time yet to be lived when the Holy Ghost (Eliezer) is seeking out a bride for the Lord Jesus Christ (Isaac).

The servant a type of the Holy Spirit has 10 camels, one for himself and 9 (fruit of the Spirit as in Galatians 5:22) loaded with gifts. See Genesis 17 and Galatians 5 for additional fruitfulness associated with the number nine.

Genesis 28:3, a curious note here on the number **nine,** it is "fruitful", the ninth word in the verse is "fruitful" and the 18th word in the verse is "multitude".

"God Almighty" Genesis 17:1 is the first mention of the phrase "Almighty God" it is where the Lord appears unto Abram and declares himself as **"Almighty God".** The word 'Almighty' appears 57 times in the scripture and all 57 of them are a reference to the Lord God. God is a trinity, he has 3 dominate attributes, he is Omnipotent (all powerful), Omniscient (all knowing), and Omnipresent (everywhere at once).

Genesis 49:1, the first use of the phrase "<u>in the last days</u>" (13 letters) 1-27 is a prophecy of the last days as it plays out for the 12 tribes of Israel. There are 67 words that appear for the first time in the bible in these 27 (3x9) verses. The prophetic chapters contain the highest number of first mention words compared to other chapters. The prophecy concerning Joseph is five verses the longest of the prophecies. **The number for "fruitfulness" is the number "nine"; Joseph just happens to be the 9th son of Jacob.**

Deuteronomy 3:11, "<u>bedstead</u>" used twice in this verse and these two occurrences are the only use of the word and emphasizes the gigantic size of the giants. The word bedstead is defined as "a frame for supporting a bed" (Webster's 1828) Og's bed was **36** (6x6) square cubits (9x4, length times width) and we can also see that 9+4= **13.**

The cubit of a man is said to be around 18 inches (3x6). 18in x 9 cubits (length) equals 162 inches; 18in x 4cubits (width) equals 72 inches; 162 plus 72 equals 234 inches; **234 divided by 13 equals 18**. Satan and his seed the Antichrist are COVERED UP with sixes and thirteens throughout the scripture.

Deuteronomy 9:9 Here again we have the requirements that are

met by the two witnesses of Revelation 11. Moses, Elijah, (1st Kings 19:7-8) and Jesus (Matthew 4). They were the only men recorded in the bible to have fasted for 40 days and nights on Mt. Horeb (Sinai).

Deuteronomy 9:9, 18 (9, 9, 9+9) these verses record the two forty day fasts that Moses completed and bore fruit of the tables of stone. Nine is the number for fruit bearing or fruitfulness.

Deuteronomy '12:6-11', the **Jews** were commanded to bring their **tithes 'of the land'** to Jerusalem and to eat them (vs.7) before the Lord where God chose to place his name. Have you taken your produce to Jerusalem lately? Are you a Jew in the land? 12:1, then you are not the person being spoken too here.

There are **seven** things that the Jews were to eat before the Lord in Jerusalem and then a tenth of their tithe, called "tithes", (Numbers 18) were given to the Levites (to all Levites not just the priests this included the women, children, and the blemished males who could not be priest) and the Levites gave a 'tenth of their tenth' to the High Priest's family.

The seven things that the Jews were to eat before the Lord are [1]burnt offerings (mandatory for sins), [2]sacrifices (mandatory for sins), [3]tithes (90% of the total, the tenth of the tithe was mandatory to support the entire tribe of Levy not just the priests but those Levites who did not qualify as a priest), [4]heave offerings (which is a tenth of the tithe Numbers 18:24-26), [5]vows, [6]freewill offerings and [7]the firstlings of the flocks and herds (mandatory).

These items were to be eaten by the Israelites in Jerusalem at the feasts mandated by the Lord, the Passover-Unleavened Bread, the feast of weeks (Pentecost) and the feast of Tabernacles see Exodus 12. All freewill offerings were only to be eaten by the priest and his family and the firstlings were to be totally consumed with fire as a burnt offering unto the Lord no man could eat it.

Seven people were designated to eat of the tithe in the gate, [1]you (the one who grew it), [2]your sons, [3]your daughters, [4]Levites, [5]strangers, [6]fatherless and [7]widows. (vs.17-18) also see Dt. 14:22-29.

The Israelites (not the gentiles) were to bring the tithe of **seven;** the (vs.17) corn, wine, oil, the firstlings, or any vows, freewill offerings, or heave offerings; and the Jews were commanded **to eat these tithes** before the Lord at Jerusalem (vs. 18) with the seven people groups listed above, the 90% of the tithe of the land was eaten by people who were NOT of the tribe of Levites or Levitical Priests, it was to be eaten by the one who grew it and their family.

The Holy Bible can sure shed a lot of light on the correct teaching of what the tithes was for and mess up a preacher or denomination with impure motives concerning the tithe.

In Nehemiah 10:38-39 the priests in Jerusalem took a tithe of the tithe (called the "tithes" in other words 10% of the 10% that was not eaten) that was brought to be eaten by the man and his family and brought it into the temple chambers and into the treasure house to make sure there was enough food for the priests and their families during the rebuilding of the nation after Nebuchadnezzar (a type of the Antichrist in the tribulation period) destroyed the city and carried the Jews away captive to Babylon.

Offerings are listed separate from the tithes because it was only the Jews that were required to tithe but anyone who wanted to give an offering either Jew or Gentile could do so. A freewill offering can be given to the Lord in any and every dispensation. The Lord Jesus said in Luke 6:38 "give" (the context of the entire chapter is **"to your enemies"**, (no amount specified, $1.00 is o.k. $10.00 is good, $25.00 is better) and it (whatsoever you give to your enemies) shall be given unto you; good measure, pressed down, and shaken together, and running over shall men give into your bosoms. For with the same measure that ye mete (no amount specified as a gift to their enemies) withal it shall be measured to you again." What he is saying is that what you give (freewill) to your enemies then shall man give back to you with an overflow.

Every sermon I have ever heard on this text (Luke 6:38 which is part of the "sermon on the mount" verses) I believe is wrongly applied to "New Testament giving" they say "give your tithe" to this church and men will give to you, that couldn't be further from the context or the correct application of what the Lord Jesus said, notice what Jesus did **not** say... "give all of your gifts to the local church and men will give it back to you", but he did say, "Give", the context insinuates to men, particularly to your enemies, because it is men that will give back to you.

The context of the chapter is significant because the Lord Jesus Christ was about to demonstrate this by giving HIMSELF **to and for his enemies** (i.e. every sinner which includes you and me) and was teaching us to do as he has done.

Jesus had nothing good to say to the religious Pharisees who would tithe down to the mint from the herb garden but had no compassion for the down and out especially those whom they considered to be their enemies. He only used the word "tithe" one time and at that time he was blasting the Pharisees for their hard-hearted hypocrisy, which, I might add, is not a very good association for the word "tithe".

Every Christian with an income is commanded by the Lord Jesus

Christ and by Paul the writer of the majority of N.T. books to "give" something, but nowhere did either one of them tell a Gentile believer to "tithe" anything to anyone, at any time.

The 11 Jewish tribes were to support their brethren the tribe of Levy and they were not to be supported by the heathen Gentiles in the land.
If God is going to support his work it will be done by his people not the world.

Deuteronomy 12, God commands the Jews 17 &number for victory) things to do when they enter the land of Israel, vs.1 [1]ye shall observe, vs.2 ye shall [2]destroy, [3]ye shall possess, vs.3 [4]ye shall overthrow, [5]break, [6]burn, [7]ye shall hew, [8]destroy, vs.5 [9]ye shall seek, [10]ye shall come, vs.6 [11]ye shall bring, vs.7 [12]ye shall eat, [13]ye shall rejoice, vs.10 [14]ye shall dwell in safety, vs11 [15]ye shall bring all I command, vs.12 [16]ye shall rejoice, vs.14 [17]ye shall offer.

God commands the Jews 4 things they are **NOT** to do vs. 4, ye shall [1]not do unto the Lord that which you do to the heathen, vs.8 [2]ye shall not do all these things, vs.13 [3]ye shall not offer up sacrifices just any place you choose, vs16 and [4]ye shall not eat the blood.

17 ¶ Thou mayest not eat within thy gates the tithe of thy corn, or of thy wine, or of thy oil, or the firstlings of thy herds or of thy flock, nor any of thy vows which thou vowest, nor thy freewill offerings, or heave offering of thine hand:

18 But thou must eat them before the LORD thy God in the place which the LORD thy God shall choose, thou, and thy son, and thy daughter, and thy manservant, and thy maidservant, and the Levite that *is* within thy gates: and thou shalt rejoice before the LORD thy God in all that thou puttest thine hands unto.

19 Take heed to thyself that thou forsake not the Levite as long as thou livest upon the earth. (have you supported any Levites lately?). **Deuteronomy 14:22-27** more teaching on the tithe that was strictly for the Jews not the Gentiles, for the children of Israel not the Church and where that food was to be eaten and by whom. See comments under chapter 12.

The Jews were to tithe all the "increase", not the gross but the net, after the seed was recovered that had been sown to produce the crop 14:23, "**And THOU shall eat** before the Lord thy God, in the place which he shall choose (Jerusalem) to place his name there, **the tithe of thy corn, of thy wine, and of thine oil, and the firstlings of thy herds and of thy flocks:** that thou mayest learn to fear the Lord thy God always". See Deuteronomy 16:9-11

The "tithe" was to be eaten by the farmer, his daughters, his sons, his menservants, his maidservants the stranger, the fatherless, the widow and the (non-priest) Levite out of that 10% that was eaten by those mentioned above 10% of that "tithe" called the "tithes" (10% of 10%) was to be given to the Temple Levites to make sure there was food in God's house. So much for the nonsense taught today by those who either don't know how to rightly divide the scripture or may have ulterior motives as to why they pervert the bible doctrine of the "tithe" without studying the scriptures to see what it says and to whom it is written.

Deuteronomy 14:28-29, at the end of every three years the tithes are to be eaten "in thy gates" i.e. the city nearest the man that grew the crops and with him was to be included the (non-priest) Levites, the strangers, the fatherless, and the widows in his city, that which is eaten by those not of his family was considered to be the "alms" spoken of in the scriptures. See **Deuteronomy 26:12, Amos 4:4**.

Deuteronomy 16:9, 10, 17 these verses echo Paul's instruction to the church age saints on how to give. See 2nd Corinthians 8:12. Moses says that the 'feast of weeks' was to be observed with 'a **freewill offering**' and no specific sacrifice except the daily lambs, for the Lamb of God was sacrificed on the Passover, there is no other sacrifice required, all of the Law was fulfilled at Calvary, and that's why Moses says 'freewill' nor a 'tithe', there is a difference in how God looks at us from the blood of the Lamb, and the filling of the Holy Ghost on the feast of weeks. No sacrifice, no tithe, just giving as the Lord hath blessed thee. They were to rejoice with **7 groups**: thou, thy family, servants, Levites, strangers, fatherless, and the widows, but notice that the 'church age' type that we are looking at there are 9 (fruit bearing, fruitful) specific individuals named. Nine is the Holy Ghost, fruitfulness number of the NT. See

Gal. (the 9th book of the NT, 5:22 (5+2+2=9) for the 9 fruits of the SPIRIT. The 9 individuals named are: thou, thy son, thy daughter, thy manservant, maidservant, the Levite, strangers, fatherless, and the widows. Nine specific individuals named in a 'church age, grace age, passage that is quoted by the Apostle to the Gentiles, Paul.

Washed in the blood at Passover, the Lamb is slain, the blood is shed, everyone who gets the blood goes on to the Holy Ghost sealing, then on to the trumpets, and then the tabernacle-ing with the Lord forever. Once the blood is accepted, the Law is complete, there is no other sacrifice, or no requirement mentioned of a tithe at the 'feast of Weeks', which is a picture of the baptism of the Holy Ghost. Amen! Give as God has blessed you!

Requite; verse 10, rejoice; verse 11, remember where you come from; verse 12.

Judges 4:13 the 9th word is 'nine'. Here Sisera, a type of 'the Antichrist' (13 letters), gathers all of the of his armies together, thinking to destroy the Israelites, but God is the one gathering the United Nations (13 letters) to defeat them at Armageddon, with one fatal blow to the head. See Zech. 12:3-5 14:14.

Judges 4:<u>13</u>, the <u>**13**</u>th word of Deborah's quote is the name '**Sisera**'.

FIRST SAMUEL: The Ninth Book of the Bible:
"Nine" is the Number of Fruit Bearing:

1st Samuel 9 contains 27 (3x9) verses and 1st Samuel is the ninth book of the King James Holy Bible.

1st Kings 17:22 is the first bible recorded event of a person being raised from the dead. Elijah the prophet performed the feat as a foreshadowing of those who will be raised from the dead during the tribulation period to show that God is authenticating his messengers. There are 9 individuals who were raised from the dead:

here, #1, widow's **son** by Elijah;

#2, 2nd Kings 4:34-35 the Shunamites **son**, and #3, 13:20 the **man** who touched Elisha's bones;

#4, Jairus' **daughter** Luke 8:52-56,

#5, Widow of Nain's **son**,

#6, John 11 **Lazarus**, by Jesus;

#7, the number for perfection was Jesus raised by God the Father and the Holy Ghost.

#8, **Dorcas** by Peter, Acts 9:40;

#9, **Eutychus** by Paul, Acts 20:9

Seven of the nine were 'male' two were 'females'.

Ezra 9, Ezra 9 is one of the great prayers of the bible. There are 3 chapters in the bible that are prayers, and they all appear in a chapter **9**. Nine is the number for fruitfulness, prayer is the most fruitful of Christian activities. See Ezra 9, Nehemiah 9, and Daniel 9 for the great prayers recorded in scripture.

Nothing bears fruit in a Christian's life like confession, and repentance.

Job 36:3, The first use of the capital "M" "**Maker**" referring to God. This capital "M" Maker is used nine (fruit bearing) times in the Bible and in the O.T. only.

Psalm 60:6-8, God is referred to 9 (3x3, trinity x trinity) ways, 3x 'I', 3x 'my', 3x mine, just an accident, yeah right.

Psalms 99 contains **9** (fruitful or fruit bearing) verses. The word "LORD" with all caps appears 7 (complete) times in this Psalm.

His **name** is holy, vs. 3; **He** is holy, vs. 5; **God** is holy, vs 9; and his **hill** is holy, vs. 9.

Psalm 99:9; 18 (2x9) words, 63 ltr (9x7)
Notice that the word "LORD" appears 7 times in the Psalm, the phrase 'the LORD our God' appears 2 times.

The 9th verse has 18 (2x9) words, there are 63 (9*7) letters.

The word 'holy' appears 4 times.

Verse 3 His name is holy, verse 5, He is holy, verse 9, God is holy, verse 9 his hill is holy.

The Lord does 9 things in the Psalm, he [1]reigneth, he [2]sitteth, he [3]establisheth equity, he [4]executeth judgment and righteousness, he [5]answered Moses and Aaron and the priests, he [6]spake to them, he [7]gave them testimonies and ordinances, he [8]forgave them, he took [9] vengence. that is a total of 9 things that the LORD did in 99:1-9.

The PEOPLE did 9 things: tremble, praise, love judgment, exalt, worship, call upon his name, they kept, exalt, worship.

There are 7 nine letter words in the Psalm: cherubims, establish, executest, footstool, ordinance, forgavest, vengeance.

verse 5 'Exalt ye the LORD our God and worship at his 'footstool' (9 letters) for he is holy. but verse 9 says Exalt the LORD our God, and worship at his HOLY HILL, so the footstool and the holy hill (Zion) are one in the same.

Psalm 103 There are a total of 31,102 verses in the word of God, the KJHB. in Psalm 103 we come to the verses that are the exact center of the KJB based on the number of verses. There are 15,551 verses from Gen. 1:1 to Psalm 103:2: there are exactly 15,551 verses from Psalm 103:3 to Rev. 22:20.

The divide occurs at the end of verse 2, and the beginning of verse 3, so, both verse 2 and 3 are the center verses in the KJB. They contain 22 words; the middle of 22 is 11, for 22 to be divided equal you have to look at the 11th and 12th word, those two words are 'HIS BENEFITS', the 11th word from the start of verse 2, and the 11th word from the end of verse 3. The King James Holy Bible middle two words are 'HIS BENEFITS', Yea Glory!

Isaiah 48:18, "Peace and righteousness" are some of the "fruit of the Spirit" which is found in Galatians 5:22, there are nine manifestations of the fruit of the Spirit. Nine is the number for fruit and fruit bearing, Holy Ghost, and prayer. Galatians chapter 5; plus, verse 22 = 27 which is 3x9. Galatians 5+2+2 = 9, Galatians has 9 letters. Galatians is the 9th book of the NT.

The term "be fruitful" appears 9 total times in the Bible. The phrase "bare fruit" has 9 letters. There is 9 months gestation period for the woman to go full term with her fruit. King James = 9 letters, Holy Bible is 9 letters. AV 1+6+1+1= 9, Holy Ghost is 9 letters.

John 14:16 tells of the "Comforter" which has 9 letters. Noah's covenant is found in Genesis 9:9-17 which is nine verses. There are 27 (3x9) books in the NT.

48:18 O that thou hadst hearkened to my commandments! then had thy peace (Gal. 5:22 But the fruit of the Spirit is love, joy, peace, ...) been as a river, and thy righteousness (Gal. 5:5, For we through the Spirit wait for the hope of righteousness by faith) as the waves of the sea:

Isaiah 59 is the "**James**" chapter of Isaiah.

The word "judgment" appears 5 times in Isaiah 59 more than any other chapter in the Bible and it appears 9 times in the five chapters of James, 2:4, 6, 13, 13, 4:4, 11, 11, 12, 5:9

59:2 But your iniquities have separated between you and your God, and your sins have hid his face from you, that he will not hear. (James 1:5-8, 4:2,3 prayer)

Daniel 2 is the longest chapter in the book with 49 verses.

Daniel 2, "secret and secrets" appears 9 times in the chapter.

Daniel 'Nine'; there are three great chapters that contain prayers of repentance and they all three are found in a chapter NINE; Ezra 9, Nehemiah 9 and here in Daniel 9. Nine is a type of 'prayer', the Holy Ghost, and fruitfulness.

Haggai 2:10, the 9th word is 'nine'.

Matthew 1:18, The number **nine** is associated in the scripture with "fruit, fruit bearing, and fruitfulness", the Holy Ghost, and prayer. The words 'Holy Ghost' (9 letters) appears 90 (10x9) times in the bible. This is the first mention of the name 'Holy Ghost', it is in verse 18 (1+8=9, and 2x9) He is only mentioned in the NT, in the OT he is called the 'Spirit'.

There are **nine** specific "fruit of the spirit" named in the **ninth** book of the New Testament; Galatians (9 letters), the address 5:22 which also equals nine, (5+2+2=9). It takes 9 months to produce a baby and all animal and insect gestations use nine as their term for producing offspring whether it be 27 weeks or 45 weeks, they are all divisible by 9, (fruit).

TAKEN FROM: Galatians 5:22, the word Holy Ghost appears 90 (10x9) times in the bible. Nine is the number given for fruit or fruit bearing. There are nine specific "fruit of the spirit" in Galatians 5:22, it takes 9 months for gestation etc.

Galatians 5:22 Galatians (**9** letters) is the **ninth** book of the N.T. and in Galatians 5:22 we find the **nine** manifestations of the "fruit of the Spirit" the address is: 5+2+2=**9** or 5+22=27 (3x9) Nine is the bible number for fruitfulness or fruit bearing. Here are some "fruitful" items that are associated with the number nine. There are 27 (3x**9**) books in the NT, (2+7=9), The phrase "Be fruitful" appears **9x** in the Bible, "bare fruit" (9 letters) appears **9x** in the bible, Genesis **9:9**-17, the Noahic covenant, consists of **9** verses were Noah is told to "be fruitful and multiply" in Genesis **9:1**. It takes **9** months for a woman to produce fruit of a child, the name "Holy Ghost" **9** ltrs appears 90 (10x9) times in the bible, in John 14:16 he is named the "Comforter" (**9** ltrs), the "King James" (**9** ltrs) "Holy Bible" (**9** ltrs) was produced in

"1611" (1 + 6 + 1 + 1 = **9**).

In 1st Corinthians 12:8-10 we have listed the **9** gifts of the Holy Spirit to the body of "believers" (**9** ltrs). Count the letters in the words: **Christian, salvation, committed, justified, satisfied, forgiving, godliness, righteous, fulfilled, repenting, scripture, doubtless, blameless, purifying, assurance, disciples, sacrifice, believers, spiritual, confessed, anointing, unspotted, believing, devotions, discerned, fortified, almsdeeds, persuaded, soundness, willingly, receiving, effectual, glorified, blessings, cleansing, encourage, dedicated, convicted, honorable, perfected, guiltless, temperate, sanctuary, conformed, abounding, submitted, behaviour, sincerity, unfeigned, faultless, crucified, peaceable, reckoning, unspotted, delivered, transform, sweetness, abundance, witnesses, volunteer, accepting, converted, affection, belonging, following, communion, labouring, reasoning, knowledge, obedience, rejoicing,** and **surrender,** they all have to do with a fruitful spirit filled life.

The phrase; capital "H" Holy, capital "S" Spirit; is found only once in the scripture at Luke 11:13. The phrase; small "h" holy with the small "s" spirit and the phrase; small "h" holy with the capital "S" Spirit appears 2 and 5 times respectively a total of 7 times in scripture whereas the phrase Holy Ghost appears 90 times (10x fruitfulness) in scripture.

Matthew 3:11 the verses with the words: "baptize" or "baptized" along with the words "Holy Ghost", are mentioned in the same verse, 9 times, 9 is the number for 'fruitfulness': "**baptize**", Matt. 3:11, Mk. 1:8, Lk. 3:16, and Jn. 1:33; "**baptized**" Mk. 1:8, Acts 1:5, 2:38, 10:47, and 11:16. It just happens to be **9** times, which is the number for "fruitfulness" and "Holy Ghost". Holy Ghost appears 90 (10x9) times in the scripture.

Matthew 9:18 There are 9 individuals who were raised from the dead:

#1, widow's **son** by Elijah;

#2, 2nd Kings 4:34-35 the Shunamites **son**, and #3, 13:20 the

man who touched Elisha's bones;

> #4, Jairus' **daughter** Matthew 9:23,
>
> #5, Widow of Nain's **son**, Luke 7:14
>
> #6, **Lazarus**, John 11 by Jesus;
>
> **#7, the number for perfection was Jesus raised by God the Father and the Holy Ghost in John 20.**
>
> #8, **Dorcas** by Peter, Acts 9:40;
>
> #9, **Eutychus** by Paul, Acts 20:9
>
> Seven of the nine were 'male' two were 'females'.

Matthew 16:21 Seven specific prophecies concerning the death, burial and resurrection of the Lord Jesus stated before it took place; let's see any modern day "prophet" do this. *go to Jerusalem, *suffer many things *suffer many things of the elders, *suffer many things of the chief priests, *suffer many things of the scribes, *be killed, *and be raised again the third day.

The number 3 is the number for the 'Trinity' and 'divine perfection'. Jesus is God in the flesh, a member of the Godhead (3x in scripture) which comprises 3 persons, the Father, Son, and Holy Ghost. **The bible records 9 (3x3) times when the Lord Jesus prophesied specific details regarding his [1]death, [2]burial, and [3]resurrection: Matthew 16:21, 17:22, 20:17 Mark 8:31, 9:31, 10:34, Luke 9:22, 18:33 and John 20:9.** Just a coincidence I'm sure! Matthew contains 3 mentions of the death, burial, and resurrection of the Lord Jesus Christ: Matthew 16:21, 17:22 and 20:17.

Matthew 18:21 here we have the 6th (man) mention in the NT of the word "seven": the context is "human (man's) reasoning about forgiveness of an offended party, the 7th (complete, perfect) and 8th (new beginning) use of the word seven is in 18:22, Jesus sets the "complete" parameters on the forgiveness issue which begins a new relationship with the offender; the 9th (fruit) context is "married" which is the fruitful connection. See Gen. 7:10 "Noah" for the 6th, 7th, 8th and 9th use of the word seven in the bible.

This coincidence also extends to the book of Mark 12:20: the 6th (man) use in Mark is "brethren" the 7th (perfect, complete) use the word seven; verse 22, is a context of "died" which is the end or completion of life; the 8th (new beginnings) use of the word is verse 23, with the mention of the "resurrection" which is the new beginning of the soul in another place.

Again, in the book of Luke 20:29: the 6th (man) use of the word seven is 7 "brother" (men), the 7th (complete) verse 31 all died; (finished, completed life), the 8th (new beginnings are in verse 33, the mention of the resurrection (new beginning).

Matthew 20:5, the first New Testament mention of the word **"ninth"** just happens to be the ninth word in the verse, and the phrase 'ninth hour' containing 9 letters, just happens to appear 9 times in the bible.
The number nine is the bible number for 'fruit'.

See Genesis 5:5 for the first mention of the word **"nine"** it also appears as the "ninth word" in that verse. Just a coincidence I'm sure, NOT!

Matthew 27:45, 2+7+4+5=18 (3x6); or 9+9. The phrase "sixth hour" appear 6 times in the bible, the phrase "ninth hour" (9 letters) appears 9 times in the bible.

Matthew 27:46; The interpretation of his words; Eli, Eli, lama sabachthani is 9 words; "My God, my God, why hast thou forsaken me?

Matthew 27:54 2+7+5+4=18 (3x6), 27+54=91 (7x13); this is the record of the first person saved "after" the death of the Lord Jesus Christ. The "Centurion" (9 letters) in a verse that equals 9+9, captain over 100 Roman soldiers, confessed **"Truly this was the Son of God"**; 7 words that will save a soul and change a generation.

Mark 15:34 the 'ninth hour' appears 9 times in the scripture, and contains 9 letters. The 9th hour is the time of the evening sacrifice,

Jesus was the sacrifice that took away the sins of the world, once and for all.

Luke 8:51 there are 7 people allowed in the room where Jairus' daughter was healed; [1]Jesus; [2]Peter; [3]James; [4]John; [5]Jairus, [6]the mother; and the [7]child.

There are **9** individuals who were raised from the dead:

#1, widow's **son** by Elijah;

#2, 2nd Kings 4:34-35 the Shunamites **son**, and #3, 13:20 the **man** who touched Elisha's bones;

#4, Jairus' **daughter** Matthew 9:23,

#5, Widow of Nain's **son**, Luke 7:14

#6, **Lazarus**, John 11 by Jesus;

#7, the number for perfection was **Jesus** raised by God the Father and the Holy Ghost in John 20.

#8, **Dorcas** by Peter, Acts 9:40;

#9, **Eutychus** by Paul, Acts 20:9

Seven of the nine were 'male' two were 'females'

Luke 23:44 (2+3+4+4=13) the sixth word in the verse is "sixth"; the phrase "sixth hour" appears 6 times in the bible. There was "darkness" over all the earth until the "ninth hour" (9 letters and appears 9 times in the bible).

John the book of **Isaiah 43:9** The word "TRUTH" appears 27 (3x9) times in John more than any other book of the Bible.

The bible records 9 specific individuals who were raised from the dead:

#1- 1st Kings 17:22 the widow of Sharaphats **son** by Elijah;

#2- 2nd Kings 4:34 the Shunamites **son** by Elisha; #3- 2nd Kings 13:20 the **man** who was let down and touched Elisha's bones;

#4- Luke 8:52 Jairus' **daughter** by The Lord Jesus; #5- Luke 7:14 widow of Nain's **son** by The Lord Jesus;

#6- John 11 **Lazarus** by The Lord Jesus;

#7- Acts 9:40 **Dorcas** by the Apostle Peter;

#8- Acts 20:9-12 **Eutychus** by the Apostle Paul.
#9- The Gospels; **The Lord Jesus Christ** by the Godhead.

John 14:16, The first use of the word "**Comforter**" (9 letters), referring to the "Holy Ghost" (9 letters), the Spirit of truth. The number nine is the number for 'prayer', 'fruit bearing' and the 'Holy Ghost'.

John 14 is the 23rd Psalm of the New Testament. The Holy Ghost (9 letters) is the Comforter (9 letters) who bears the 9 fruit of the spirit found in Galatians 5:22. Galatians (**9** letters) is the **ninth** book of the N.T. and in Galatians 5:22 we find the nine manifestations of the "fruit of the Spirit" the address of the nine manifestations is Gal. 5+2+2=**9**. Nine is the bible number for fruitfulness or fruit bearing, prayer, and the Holy Ghost. Here are some "fruitful" items that are associated with the number nine.
There are 27 (3x**9**) books in the N.T.,
"Be fruitful" appears **nine** times in the Bible,
"bare fruit" (9 letters) appears **9x** in the bible,
Genesis **9:9**-17 the Noahic covenant consists of **9** verses were Noah is told to "be fruitful and multiply" in Genesis **9:1**.
It takes **9** months for a woman to produce fruit of a child,
the name "Holy Ghost" equals **9** letters and appears 90 (10x9) times in the bible, he is named the "Comforter" (**9** ltrs),
the "King James" (**9** ltrs) "Holy Bible" (**9** ltrs) was produced in "1611" (1+6+1+1 = **9**).
In I Cor. 12:8-10 we have listed the **9** gifts of the Holy Spirit to the body of "believers" (**9** ltrs).

John 15, the "**fruit**" chapter; the word "fruit" appears 8 times, more than any other chapter in the bible. Found in this passage are the phrases: "more fruit"; "he purgeth"; "much fruit"; "bear fruit"; "abide in me"; "and I in you"; "in the vine"; "I loved you"; "in his love"; "my friends"; "give it you"; all phrases contain 9 letters; 9 is the number of fruitfulness. See Gal. 5:22 (5+2+2=9)

John 15:4, "abide" appears 9x (number of fruit bearing) in John.

There are 9 months for gestation period,
9 manifestations of the fruit of the spirit in Galatians 5;
Noah was commanded to be fruitful in Genesis 9.
See Gal. 5:22 for additional "nines".

John 15:6 "Abiding" is not for "salvation" but for "discipleship" verse 8. If a believer refuses to walk in a disciplined life in Christ; then he will not be fruitful, therefore he or she will be cast forth; wither; and discarded; without ever bearing fruit of discipleship. This is not a salvation verse; it is a fruit bearing verse; a life of surrender, consecration, perseverance, dedication, willing surrender, thankful obedience, and holiness which "bears fruit".

Staying close to the bosom of Christ; and abiding in him; will allow him to produce fruit that glorifies the Father; vs 9.

John 15:26 The Comforter (9 letters) is: the third person of the Godhead. He is the "Holy Ghost" (appears 90x only in the NT); He proceeds from the Father; He is the "Spirit of truth"; He testifies, magnifies, and glorifies, Jesus Christ,
Jn. 4:24, He is the Spirit of God, who is a Spirit;
Gen. 1:2, He was active in **creation,**

2nd Tim, He was active in **inspiration,**
John 16:9, He is active in **conviction,**
John 1:12, He is active in **regeneration,**

1st Peter 1:12, He is active in **sanctification,**
Rom. 8:11, He was active in **Christ's resurrection,**
Rom. 8:11, He will be active in **my resurrection,**
The Holy Ghost: circumcises, fills, seals, teaches, guides, reproves, rebukes, disciplines, and sanctifies every sinner, who comes to Jesus Christ for the salvation of his soul; by grace through faith in his finished work on Calvary.

John 16:8 the three works of the Comforter; REPROVE, REPROVE, REPROVE. Comforter, 9 letters, Holy Ghost, 9 letters.

John 16:13, 14 here are 9 (spiritual fruitful) personal references made of the Comforter showing that he is a "person" of the Godhead, not just an influence; when **HE** is come, **He** will guide, **He** shall not speak of **Himself**, **He** shall hear, **He** shall speak, **He** will shew, **He** shall glorify me, and **He** shall receive of mine.

Acts 3:1 the hour of prayer, 'the ninth hour', 3 pm. The phrase 'ninth hour' appears 9 times in the scripture and contains 9 letters.

Nine is the number for; prayer, fruit bearing, and the 'Holy Ghost' (9 letters).

Acts 9:1-9 Nine verses here recording the conversion of the greatest Christian that ever lived. He was the 13th Apostle, he penned 13 Church Age Epistles, and 1 Hebrew Epistle. The salvation of 'by grace through faith' comes out of this chapter 9 of Acts. Saul, is born again and takes the name of Paul, a new identity in Christ.

Acts 9 (The number for fruitfulness) we have the conversion of the Apostle Paul, the Apostle to the Gentiles, without doubt the most fruitful Christian that ever lived. Paul was the 13th Apostle who wrote 13 Church epistles (letters) and one Jewish epistle called The Book of Hebrews.

There are 9 individuals who were raised from the dead:

#1, widow's **son** by Elijah;

#2, 2nd Kings 4:34-35 the Shunamites **son**, and #3, 13:20 the **man** who touched Elisha's bones;

#4, Jairus' **daughter** Matthew 9:23,

#5, Widow of Nain's **son**, Luke 7:14

#6, **Lazarus**, John 11 by Jesus;

#7, the number for perfection was Jesus raised by God the Father and the Holy Ghost in John chapter 20.

#8, **Dorcas** by Peter, Acts 9:40;

#9, **Eutychus** by Paul, Acts 20:9

Seven of the nine were 'male' two were 'females'

Acts 10:3 Cornelius saw a vision about the "ninth hour" (9 letters) and the word "ninth" is the ninth word in the verse.

Acts 10:29 is the 9th and last appearance of the phrase "ninth hour" (9 letters) in the scripture.

Acts 20:9, There are 9 individuals who were raised from the dead:

#1, 1st Kings 17:22; the widow's **son** by Elijah;

#2, 2nd Kings 4:34-35 the Shunamites **son**, and #3, 13:20 the **man** who touched Elisha's bones;
#4, Jairus' **daughter** Matthew 9:23,
#5, Widow of Nain's **son**, Luke 7:14
#6, **Lazarus**, John 11 by Jesus;
#7, the number for perfection was Jesus raised by God the Father and the Holy Ghost in John 20.
#8, **Dorcas** by Peter, Acts 9:40;
#9, **Eutychus** by Paul, Acts 20:9
Seven of the nine were 'male' two were 'female'.

1st Corinthians 12:8-10; 9 is the number of fruitfulness or fruit bearing.
The spiritual **gifts**, given by the Holy Spirit to believers are 9 in number, they are: [1]wisdom; [2]word of knowledge; [3]faith; [4]gifts of healing; [5]working of miracles; [6]prophecy; [7]discerning of spirits; [8]divers tongues; and the [9]interpretation of tongues.
There are also 9 **fruit** of the Spirit given in Gal. 5:22 (5+2+2=9).

1st Corinthians 12:28-13:1, a list of 9 (fruitful) things God has set in the N.T. Church. *Apostles, *prophets, *teachers, *miracles, *healings, *helps, *governments, *diversities of tongues; and *charity.

Galatians: The 48th Book of the Bible: the 9th book of the NT
Galatians (**9** letters) is the **ninth** book of the N.T. and in Galatians 5:22 we find the nine manifestations of the "fruit of the Spirit" the address of the nine manifestations is 5+2+2=**9** or 5+22=27 which is 3x9. Nine is the bible number for fruitfulness or fruit bearing.

Here are some "fruitful" items that are associated with the number nine. There are 27 (3x**9**) books in the N.T., "Be fruitful" appears **nine** times in the Bible, "bare fruit" appears **9x**, Genesis **9:9**-17 the Noahic covenant consists of **9** verses were Noah is told to "be fruitful and multiply" in Genesis **9**:1. It takes **9** months for a woman to produce fruit of a child, the name "Holy Ghost" equals **9** letters and appears 90 (10x9) times in the bible, he is named the "Comforter" (**9** ltrs), the "King James" (**9** ltrs) "Holy Bible" (**9** ltrs) was produced in "1611" (1+6+1+1 = **9**). In I Cor. 12:8-10 we have listed the **9** gifts of the Holy Spirit to the body of "believers" (**9** ltrs). Genesis 24 the longest chapter in Genesis (the church age is the longest dispensation to be lived thus far) is the chapter where Eliezer the servant is a type of the Holy Spirit searching for a bride for Isaac. He has 10 camels one for himself and 9 loaded down with gifts for the bride, the body of Christ.

Galatians 5:22, the word Holy Ghost appears 90 (10x9) times in the bible: Nine is the number given for fruit or fruit bearing: There are nine specific "fruit of the spirit" in Galatians 5:22, it takes 9 months for gestation: Galatians (**9** letters) is the **ninth** book of the N.T. and in Galatians 5:22 we find the **nine** manifestations of the "fruit of the Spirit": the address is: 5+2+2=**9** or 5+22=27 (3x9):

Nine is the bible number for fruitfulness or fruit bearing. Here are some "fruitful" items that are associated with the number nine: There are 27 (3x**9**) books in the NT, 2+7=9: the phrase "Be fruitful" appears **9x** in the Bible: "bare fruit" (9 letters) appears **9x** in the bible: Gen. 17, Abraham was 99 and Sarah was 90 at the conception of the miracle baby; Isaac: Genesis **9:9**-17 the Noahic covenant consists of **9** verses were Noah is told to "be fruitful and multiply" in Genesis **9**:1: It takes **9** months for a woman to produce fruit of a child: the name "Holy Ghost" contains **9** ltrs and appears 90 (10x9) times in the bible: in John 14:16 he is named the "Comforter" (**9** ltrs): the "King James" (**9** ltrs) "Holy Bible" (**9** ltrs) was produced in "1611" (1+6+1+1 = **9**): In Exodus 25 the ninth item named for the Tabernacle was the "Oil" type of the Holy:

In 1st Corinthians 12:8-10 we have the **9** gifts listed of the Holy Spirit to the body of "believers" (**9** ltrs). Count the letters in these words "**salvation, Christian, righteous, sacrifice, believers, dedicated, honorable, and crucified**" they all have to do with a fruitful spirit filled life.

Galatians 5:22-26 the "fruit of the Spirit" verses contain 63 words which equals 7x9 describing the 9, "Fruit of the Spirit". Just a fluke I'm sure.